Gôd & Marriage

The Original Plan

God & Marriage

The Original Plan

Folayemi Godswill-Oko

God and Marriage
The Original Plan

ISBN: 978-81-19524-51-8

First published in India in 2024 by Exceller Books,
An imprint of GE Group
Address: G1, Dream Apartment, Degree College Road, Belgharia, Kolkata, 700056, India

www.excellerbooks.com

Acknowledgement

All thanks are due to the writer's resource, the Almighty God, who is the genius behind it all.

Dedication

This book is dedicated to the author of marriage and also to all the women around the world, both married and single, old and young.

References

The Holy Bible

King James Version

And

Personal Experiences of Some Women of Faith

Table of Contents

Introduction

He made the first man and, at the right time, a woman from the man. He created them to eradicate loneliness. Genesis 2:18, 21-24.

According to Sapna Dhandh Sharma, there is a purpose for every action. God has a purpose for creating man, and He likewise has a purpose for the union of man and wife. God's purpose for marriage is clearly spelt out in His Word.

Marriage is beautiful when its purpose and characteristics are known and implemented. This book, with the help of the Holy Spirit, has examined marriage from God's perspective.

My prayer is that God himself will speak to you and me through this book; that He will give us direction where needed, heal us where we hurt, strengthen our feeble knees and give us the grace for success as women, wives, mothers, sisters and builders of homes in Jesus name. (Amen)

When I started this book, I was lying on a hospital bed during the pregnancy of one of my boys. I had been in that bed for days and had to read several books, watch movies, sleep and, of course, eat.

Nevertheless, while my routine continued unaltered for nine days, the tenth day was different. I received inspiration for this book. I lay there trying to read or sleep—whichever came first—when the urge to pick up my writing materials struck me.

I resisted for a while, but the more I hesitated, the more the ideas and inspiration kept rolling in as though I had already started writing. Then the Spirit of the Lord brought a passage of the scripture to my mind: Hebrews 2:2-3. At this point, I got off the bed and drew out my book and pen. What follows is what God has in stock for us in this book: "God and Marriage -The Woman".

Hebrews 2:2-3
"For if the word spoken by angels was steadfast, and every transgression and disobedience received a just recompense of reward;"

"How shall we escape, if we neglect so great salvation; which at the first began to be spoken by the Lord, and was confirmed unto us by them that heard him..."

"Marriage is an institution ordained by God Himself and it started in the Garden of Eden..."

Genesis 2:18
"And God said, it is not good for the man to be alone."

God saw the need for a helper in the home. God saw the need for family, He saw the need for relationships, and He saw the need for marriage. From verses 24-25 of the same

Genesis 2, God, in a short form, defined the term "marriage".

In this book, we will be looking at some of the important terms in God's definition of marriage.

Genesis 2:24-25

"Therefore shall a man leave his father and his mother, and shall cleave unto his wife: and they shall be one flesh."

"And they were both naked, the man and his wife, and were not ashamed."

The bold words: **'leaves'**, **'cleaves'**, **'naked'**, and **'not ashamed'**, in the passage above which will lead us into the foundation of marriage - the reason why some will stand till the coming of the Lord and the reason why some are and are still falling apart. These words or phrases will be considered one after the other in relation to what God says in His word concerning them.

Wait a Minute

Before you go further into the book and what God's plan for your marriage is, take a minute to say this short prayer. Dear God, thank You for who You have made me and for the wonderful husband You have given me (or will give me). I know You brought us together for Your own purpose and Your purpose You will accomplish. As I read on, create in me a new heart and renew Your Spirit within me to take up my duties as a true helper and a virtuous woman in my husband's life and home in Jesus' name (Amen).

As simple as the above prayer might seem when prayed in truth and with a sincere heart, it gives the grace you need to help achieve the aforementioned points in God's marriage definition.

Section I

Part I: Leave

In a literal term, the word 'leave' means to move from one point to another. It often refers to location or position: leave your house to go somewhere else, leave a job to pick up another.

Leaving in God's terms refers to the same thing; just that this time, when God says leave, the fellow receiving such direction is heading for a location and set for divine allocation.

The Bible is filled with several examples where God directs an individual to leave. We will consider some of these people, their reactions to the instruction, and the outcome.

Abraham: Genesis 12:1
"Now the LORD had said unto Abram, Get thee out of thy country, and from thy kindred, and from thy father's house, unto a land that I will shew thee:"

Elijah: 1Kings 17:3
"Get thee hence, and turn thee eastward, and hide thyself by the brook Cherith that is before Jordan."

The woman from Shunem: 2 Kings 8:1-2

"Then spake Elisha unto the woman, whose son he had restored to life, saying, Arise, and go thou and thine household, and sojourn wheresoever thou canst sojourn: for the Lord hath called for a famine; and it shall also come upon the land seven years."

"And the woman arose, and did after the saying of the man of God: and she went with her household, and sojourned in the land of the Philistines seven years."

Joseph: Matthew 2:13

"And when they were departed, behold, the angel of the Lord appeareth to Joseph in a dream, saying, Arise, and take the young child and his mother, and flee into Egypt, and be thou there until I bring thee word: for Herod will seek the young child to destroy him."

When God says "leave", He has made provision ready for you in the new location. In the same way, when God told man to leave, He had provided for him a wife, not just a wife but a person with the capability of being unto him a father and a mother. God says, "Leave your father and your mother", which does not mean God wants to strip the man of parental care; rather, He has deposited in the wife "the potential of parenthood". Thus, in her, he finds all and misses nothing.

I have heard wives say things like, "I clean up after him, tell him how to do this and that, I am not his mother, I am tired of him". This is not supposed to be this way. If he was perfect with no need for help, there wouldn't be a need for you, there would be no need for a helpmate, and God chose you specifically as his helpmate because you are the best for this position. In this case, if you give up on him, you have simply given up on your God-given responsibility as a wife.

When a man leaves his father and mother, he leaves his first and biological family. The wife then becomes his new family before the children start coming in. When a wife then abandons her responsibility to this man, he is left in a vacuum, and he is tempted to be in need of "spoil."

Proverbs 31:10-11

"Who can find a virtuous woman? For her price is far above rubies."

"The heart of her husband doth safely trust in her, so that he shall have no need of spoil."

The verses above explain the worth of a virtuous woman and how, if the value is not expressed, it can affect her husband. It says "her husband… trust". If a wife manifests her stand as a virtuous wife, submits herself and is conscious of the fact that her husband had left all (family) for her, treats him in like manner, he will be rest assured in her arms, he will trust her, he will not have reasons to need the spoil. Spoil here refers to waywardness, extramarital relationships, drunkenness, loss of integrity, etc.

I am not saying the man is the only one who leaves. The point is that in the place of marriage and keeping a home, most of the responsibility for keeping that home rests on the helpmate.

Proverbs 14:1

"Every wise woman buildeth her house: but the foolish plucketh it down with her hands."

The Bible does not say that a "wise man" builds; it says that every "wise woman" builds. It's the duty of the wife to build the home, to stabilise the relationship between herself and her husband, herself and her children, and then a family with extended family. It is when this is properly done that she will claim God's blessings in Proverbs 3:35

Proverbs 3:35

"The wise shall inherit glory: but shame shall be the promotion of fools."

If she is a wise woman who builds her house, then she is due for the glory meant for the wise. Are you wise?

Prayer

"Father Lord, I come before You to ask for grace to be wise. Let wisdom proceed from my heart, through my mouth and to everyone around me. Let me not be a carrier of folly in the name of Jesus. Amen."

God said the man shall leave his father and mother. Some wives have misunderstood this part. God did not say he should neglect them or never contact or communicate with them, which is the expectation of some wives who want all attention directed to them after marriage or who simply want to use the marriage to get rid of their "overbearing" mothers-in-law while trying to attract all attention to themselves. I have spoken to women who say, "At least God said he should leave his father and mother", a big mistake. The same bible says the only way to live long is to honour your parents.

Exodus 20:12

"Honour thy father and thy mother: that thy days may be long upon the land which the LORD thy God giveth thee."

So, if you want your husband to live long, don't ask him to ignore and despise by not communicating and caring for his parents.

To make living worthwhile, we need to master acceptance. Take, for instance, you told a friend living on another continent that you would be visiting for a couple of weeks during your annual work leave. Your friend sounded enthusiastic and even told you all the plans she has in stock for you, the places you would visit, the people you would get to meet, the new delicious local dishes from traditional restaurants, etc. You were so full of hope and excitement; this would surely be a nice time. You travel to your dream vacation land and get to your friend's door, but she refuses to let you in or allow you into the house and abandons you there. This is what happens when the man leaves, and the wife does not accept him through her attitude.

I perceive in my spirit that someone is saying: how could this be? I love him; I married him, so how can I treat him like he's nothing?

- My friend, when you nag, it's not acceptance.
- When you correct out of superiority and not love, it's not acceptance.
- When you refuse to identify with him publicly because he is less educated, has a paid job, and thus earns less.
- Deny him food or sex as a means of punishment.
- Talk about him harshly with friends and not cover/protect his interests.
- Treat his family, especially his mother, with contempt.
- Then you are not accepting him. You are the same as the friend described earlier, who neglected her friend who came to her on vacation. Then, you are not what the Bible calls the virtuous wife or the wise woman.

Prayer

Dear Lord, I ask for the strength to be who you want me to be. I receive the strength to be wise and virtuous. Lord, I admit that sometimes I am weak, tired, and maybe confused, but please give me the strength and grace to fulfil my purpose in Jesus' name. Amen.

Part II: Cleave

The second point in the definition of marriage is CLEAVE. Cleave here means to join, to be added to something else, to stick together or to attach. This section better explains the relevance of accepting one's partner. If cleaving here actually means to join, it settles the reason why God says in the later part of the verse that both the man and his wife will become one flesh.

Genesis 2:24b

"Therefore shall a man leave his father and his mother, and shall cleave unto his wife: **and they shall be one flesh.**"

They shall be one flesh, they shall be the same; they might have been two entities but are now one, their lives are considered as one, and none is perfect without the other - "... and they shall be one flesh".

When you say your partner has a bad habit and, therefore, you are ashamed of him/her, then you are referring to yourself, you are ashamed of yourself, and you are not accepting yourself. Little wonder how pain and depression set in gradually. How can you hate yourself and expect to be happy?!

Jesus being one with His disciples, having taught them his ways, walked with them all the way, shown them miracles that had left them marvelled and above all shared his body and blood with them; when Judas betrayed Jesus, he was detached from the "body" and his life did not remain the same again, he died shamefully.

Act 1:18-20

"Now this man purchased a field with the reward of iniquity; and falling headlong, he burst asunder in the midst, and all his bowels gushed out."

"And it was known unto all the dwellers at Jerusalem; insomuch as that field is called in their proper tongue, Aceldama, that is to say, The field of blood."

"For it is written in the book of Psalms, Let his habitation be desolate, and let no man dwell therein: and his bishopric let another take."

Jesus also confessed that He and the Father are one - the reason why he would not do anything he had not received of the Father.

John 17:11

"God still requires the same from us today. When we detach ourselves from a God-given assignment, which our marriage is of course inclusive, we break the hedge."

Ecclesiastes 10:8

"He that diggeth a pit shall fall into it; and whoso breaketh a hedge, a serpent shall bite him."

Your home is for you to protect. Your partner's interests must be protected in the face of your own family and friends. Do not take pleasure in discussing your weaknesses with a third party, even when things go wrong between you. Throughout the whole chapter of John 17, Jesus prayed for His disciples. We are expected to likewise pray for our partners. Pray and not criticize.

I will share the story of a friend whose husband works as a computer specialist. After their marriage, he got a job in Saudi Arabia and moved there. She joined him, but not long after, he lost his job, but he soon got another job in Ireland. Initially, she did not want to follow him as these movements were taking a toll on her career, but after much persuasion from friends and family, she followed him. Their stay in Ireland ended after he lost his job six months later. At this point, they both decided to stay in Poland, live and work in a city where they both have opportunities to get good jobs. A week after they moved into the new place in Poland, he announced that he had gotten a job in California and would like to move there irrespective of their agreement and plan, and he was to move in less than a week.

Now, what should she do? Leave him or cleave to him? Totally abandon her career and keep moving wherever he goes? Situations like this need prayers; they need you to be on your knees and seek the face of the author of marriage.

However, it is better mentally, psychologically and emotionally to cleave than to separate.

Part III: Naked

Openness, vulnerability, no secrets, no hidden intentions or agenda; this is God's idea of nakedness. Let's go back to the Garden of Eden. After man sinned, he noticed he was naked and sought for coverage. When sin creeps in, we try to cover the nakedness, we are no longer open, we begin to hide under bushes like Adam and Eve did - the same person we were free with before suddenly becomes our object of shame.

In a God-family setting, the need for openness is expedient. In any family that would survive, no secrets must be allowed, either secrets held before or after marriage. Total openness between the partners is important. The Bible says love covers a multitude of sins. If you love your partner, you will forgive him as Jesus does your sins on a daily basis just because He loves you.

1John 4:18

"There is no fear in love; but perfect love casteth out fear: because fear hath torment. He that feareth is not made perfect in love."

Genesis 2:25

"And they were both naked, the man and his wife, and were not ashamed."

1 Peter 4:8

"And above all things have fervent charity among yourselves: for charity shall cover the multitude of sins."

Let's take a look at two families in the Bible, the first being Lot - Abraham's nephew. He was saved from the destruction that came on Sodom and Gomorrah (Genesis 19). However, his wife, who had left the city, still had her eyes and mind on the beauty and excitement of Sodom and Gomorrah. She disobeyed the order they received: "Look not behind thee"; she looked back and became a pillar of salt.

Genesis 19:17

"And it came to pass, when they had brought them forth abroad, that he said, Escape for thy life; look not behind thee, neither stay thou in all the plain; escape to the mountain, lest thou be consumed..."

Genesis 19:26

"But his wife looked back from behind him, and she became a pillar of salt."

Her mind was not with her husband. Had she told her husband her wish to look back, he would have protected her against it, he would have prevented her from destroying herself. On the contrary, she kept her hidden intention in her dealings with her husband, she was not naked.

Are you naked in your relationship with your husband? Is the communication between you secret-free?

Another crucial factor of being naked in marriage is finance. Most of the reasons for problems in the home can be related to financial issues. Both parties must be naked. You should be able to know how much your partner has in their account and work together to secure it for the future or invest it rather than lavishing it on irrelevant things.

Open up to your partner about the flow of cash in the family. When there is abundance, sufficiency or scarcity, do not hide any. Some women are eager to relate to the need for money, but when they get some extra cash, they keep it a secret. No secret must be allowed.

Part IV: Not Ashamed

"...And they were naked and not ashamed."

When God said "Not ashamed", He meant it in every sense.

This component will be divided into two parts: physical and other.

Physically not ashamed

God knew they were naked, but the man and his wife, Eve, didn't come to this realisation until sin came in.

Genesis 2:25

"And they were both naked, the man and his wife, and were not ashamed."

Genesis 3:7

"And the eyes of them both were opened, and they knew that they were naked; and they sewed fig leaves together, and made themselves aprons."

The passages above show that they had both been naked all along, and there was no shame in that nakedness. However, when disobedience, blame, and sin got into that nakedness, it took up a new character: SHAME.

Reasoning 1

They were the only people in the garden; who were they covering for?

Reasoning 2

Let us assume they were covering for each other even though they already saw each other naked, they were even both naked at the point of the new discovery. So, what was the point of the covering? Nonetheless, they still went ahead and sewed fig leaves for covering.

True story (Woman 1)

I feared to see a man looking at me naked. He is my husband, but I am always ashamed. I would not shower with him out of shame of him seeing me naked; I would even lock the door of the room while dressing up. At night, while in bed, I would always insist the light be turned off. I wallowed in shame against the will of the master of marriage.

Facts behind physical shame

Fact 1: My Body

My Shape: I am not beautiful enough. I am too slim, too fat, too much of this, lack of that.

My skin: My skin is not even. I have got scars. I had some surgeries and the scars would not go away.

'They were naked but not ashamed'. He is your husband, your body is his.

1 Corinthians 7:4

"The wife hath not power of her own body, but the husband: and likewise also the husband hath not power of his own body, but the wife."

Packaging, as people call it, may apply to your friends, colleagues, or even siblings but not your spouse. Not your spouse because you have been made one – naked, but not ashamed.

True story (Woman 1 continues)

I fought to be free, I love my husband and hate to see him suffer with me. My pain grew as I realised how sad my husband feels about my condition. At that point, I decided to seek for help. Man failed, psychologist would not help, but God was there, he was just there waiting for me to acknowledge Him.

I finally did, I went back to the owner of me and my marriage. I sought for the help of the porter, I allowed my self be broken, I let down the walls, I broke through my fears and shame. He healed me, How? I do not know but He did it. There is truly balm in Gilead.

Fact 2: Trauma (History)

Another reason for shame is history. So many women have been abused in different ways. Abuses such as rape, molestation, and beating can cause shame in marriage. This type of abuse drills into the soul of the victim and rips off the strength of her mind, leaving her weak and scared. Sometimes, the victim puts up a bold look and acts strong, but the pain remains fresh.

The unpleasant scenes play back when she is with her partner - she remembers the pain, and pleasure gives way to shame.

There Is a Balm in Gilead

Sisters, do not stay in that place of pain, in that place of sorrow. They might have taken your body, but do not give up your soul.

Take a conscious decision to pull back your body and soul in prayers and practical effort. Discuss how you feel with your partner. Discuss what you think while you both gradually and consciously fight against the shame in your marriage.

Obadiah 1:17

"But upon mount Zion shall be deliverance, and there shall be holiness; and the house of Jacob shall possess their possessions."

Matthew 18:19-20

"Again I say unto you, That if two of you shall agree on earth as touching anything that they shall ask, it shall be done for them of my Father which is in heaven."

"For where two or three are gathered together in my name, there am I in the midst of them."

Jeremiah 29:11

"For I know the thoughts that I think toward you, saith the Lord, thoughts of peace, and not of evil, to give you an expected end."

2Timothy 1:7

"For God hath not given us the spirit of fear; but of power, and of love, and of a sound mind."

Let us say this prayer:

My Father and my Lord, thank you for Your peace in the midst of my storms. Thank you for your strength, which has replaced my weaknesses. Thank You for the blood of Jesus shed for my sake. I cast all my cares on You, oh Lord. Please help me, and give me your strength to withstand and overcome all my worries and pains. Let me enjoy the gift of a sound mind. Let my past pass away, and let my future be beautifully wrapped in Your love and mercy in Jesus' name.

Section II

Life Experiences

This section contains a few of the life experiences of some women in marriage. Marriage, they say, "is a school of experience of its own." A lot of people have gone in and out; some have determined to simply endure it just to avoid the shame of separation either because of their custom or religious belief, some endure just to cater for their children, some endure because there is simply no other choice for them, some enjoy it because it is their dream marriage and even thought there might be challenges, they overcome them and move on.

Whichever of these categories and more you belong, one certain thing is that you are not alone. You are not the first person in this situation and sure will not be the last.

Follow me as we explore the lives of some women of faith out there who have been bent but not broken, who have been hit but not hurt, who have found the strength in their marriages.

With respect to the privacy of the women who have shared their experiences on this page, no name will be mentioned, but the stories will be shared.

Woman 2: Pain of Barrenness

I was newly born again; I knew very little about life in Christ; I just wanted to love God, find a life partner and live my life.

In the local church which I attended, a brother walked up to me one day and asked if we could be prayer partners. I agreed, and we started meeting in my office at mid-day for prayers. I liked the way he spoke in tongues and that was what I held on to. After a while, he proposed, I agreed, and all through, with the help of the Pastor, we got married.

My husband started having extramarital affairs shortly after marriage, or maybe I should say they were relationships which were there and continued into our marriage; he was doing it publicly that friends and loved ones started calling in to say they saw my husband in town with one woman or the other. At one point, he decided to also introduce me to one of the ladies as his sister, which made the lady trust and confide in me to the point that she would come to my office to tell me what was going on between herself and my husband/brother. You would ask why I didn't tell her the truth, why I didn't fight; I had my own inner struggles. I was afraid of adding any other problem to my life, so I resolved to be silent and pray in my secret place. What are your own struggles? You might ask? I had no child. I tried, and we both did, but I could not get pregnant; my in-laws had started calling in to ask why. I was already sitting on the why-aren't-you-pregnant-yet hot seat, and there was no power left to fight. After a while, The lady got pregnant for him and decided to terminate the pregnancy because my husband had promised her marriage but not with pregnancy. I was the confidant of the lady and, unfortunately, was fed with all the juicy details.

The lack of children in the marriage lasted for seven years. It was seven years of pain, worry, humiliation, cheating and many more. I went to several churches for prayers (some of which were direct instructions from my mother-in-law), fasted several times, and cried severally, however, through it all, I kept asking God for mercy.

Even though at the time, the only thing that made sense was for me to leave the marriage because my husband kept cheating and not caring even monetary wise. I stayed, I held on to my faith, I believed he was my husband and it was just a wind in our marriage. The wind blew away and after 7 years, God blessed us with a baby Boy; Michael.

What I did and how those years passed, only God could tell. I only know His grace was there for me.

Woman 3: How I survived three decades of marital abuse

This testimony is meant to strengthen every woman out there battling with marital abuse. I got married at 25, and I am now in my early 60s. Being married for almost four decades was a great experience, and many people like me were not so lucky to pull through. By next year, my husband and I will be celebrating our 37th year of marriage.

My marriage of 37 years had actually experienced 30 years of struggles, pain, unforgettable sad moments and periods of shame. We moved so swiftly from that couple that professed forever love on the altar of marriage to a couple that intentionally inflicted pain on each other. We totally forgot the word love, and we replaced it with hatred and extreme detestation of each other.

The children unfortunately grew up in such a hostile environment, but at a stage, they all left home, and I was left at home with him and the physical, emotional and psychological abuse we both brought upon each other.

You must be imagining right now the series of beautiful and ugly experiences I must have had, knowing that marriage is not exactly a bed of roses. The truth is that the ugly experiences I had far outweighed the beautiful ones. Well, the important thing is that I pulled through. I am a survivor of both physical and emotional abuse in marriage. My husband and I are still together, and we hope to be together for many more years.

You might be wondering how the miracle must have happened; I strongly believe that miracles don't happen without prayers, and the results we see are the very answers to prayers.

When I sensed that the battle was becoming too fierce, wisdom demanded separation for a while, which I believed was essential for the sanity of both and for us to individually seek God's face and figure out how badly we have both allowed the devil into our home. I decided to fight the battle on my knees while I monitored and prayed for my marriage from afar.

Another thing we did to stop the situation was inviting both his family and mine to a meeting where we could discuss the problems openly, knowing that such problems thrive in secrecy. We also had discussions with our children, who were also not in any way satisfied with the state of our home. We promised the family and children we would change. We thought at the time that we could do that by mere determination.

For over two years, we had struggled to change. That was the point when I appreciated the difficulty involved in making efforts to change by determination. I realised that change especially in marriage is actually impossible without the help of God our maker and the author of Marriage. Although our efforts to change met with one form of defeat or another, we consistently prayed and made efforts. Our children also prayed and made efforts to help us until the miracle finally happened.

We finally became one as God desired. It took a long, but we got there.

42

Woman 4: Marriage needs more than love to thrive

You probably must have heard that love is important in marriage; yes, however, there are more factors needed to make it work. God is the MAIN FACTOR; there is no negotiation, and in God comes the other factor, which is simplified in the fruit of the spirit. Patience, kindness, gentleness, meekness, and tolerance are all important.

I can state this categorically because my marriage is a show of God in a family. I am not so much of a writer, so I am not sure I can effectively write all that happened, but it was painful, it was black, and it was obviously not Godly. I wanted to run away as far as possible; my husband was also thinking in the same line; none of us were taking our children into consideration.

It started suddenly, love no longer matter, I started feeling disgusted by my husband and everything he does, I knew it was wrong but I could not help myself. There were times that I have the strong urge to pray and cast the devil out of my home but I wouldn't because I was bitter because my husband was taking me for granted and even though I am in marriage, I felt alone, unappreciated and used.

I simply allowed myself to feel so comfortable in the dark place, a place where no child of God should be, a place where I was totally vulnerable to attacks and dictates of the devil.

One day, the tide turned. I don't know how, but all I remember was that even when I was in a dark place, God never left; His mercy fought HARD for me. I would always pray even when I knew God could not answer my prayers in that state. I would read the Bible even when I knew there would not be any inspiration, and God fought, dragged me out, brought me back to light, and washed my heart clean.

When he was working on me, he was also working on my husband. Finally, we met in His arms, back to safety. My friends, only God could have saved my marriage from that storm.

Epilogue

Dear Readers,

Dear readers, thank you for taking the time to read through this book and I sincerely hope you have been blessed. Our homes are blessed and secured in His love and mercy.

The stories here might have touched your heart somehow or the scripture might have ministered to you one way or the other, you probably might have seen yourself or your home in this book, or your case is totally different; whichever way it is, remember to bring it all to God in prayers. God cares and wants to see us happy.

Stay connected to the source of strength, and never let go. Fight your battles on your knees and through your praises.

Remember, your spouse is not perfect, and neither are you.

"When we see Him, we shall be like Him." 1 John 3:2.

Stay Blessed!